The (almost) Blank Journal

A Daily Journal to Inspire Clarity and Creativity

Virginia Beach Art Gym
www.vbArtGym.com

The (almost) Blank Journal

A Daily Journal to Inspire Clarity and Creativity

Created by
Maggie Kerrigan

Published by
Virginia Beach Art Gym
Virginia Beach, VA

The (almost) Blank Journal
A Daily Journal to Inspire Clarity and Creativity

Published by Virginia Beach Art Gym

Visit us at
www.vbArtGym.com

ISBN-13: 978-1492925439
ISBN-10: 1492925438

Introduction

What is your reason for daily writing? Professional development? Personal therapy? Individuals have many different motivations for journaling. This journal is designed to help you achieve *your own* goals through your writing.

You might ask, "Why this journal? Why not a blank book?" This journal provides you a balance between a fully blank book and a fully choreographed year of writing. Creative people often benefit from some basic structure in order to function at their best. Likewise, highly structured people benefit from ideas and suggestions that stretch them out of their comfort zones. *The (almost) Blank Journal* gives you a balance of structure and openness within which to express your dreams and ideas.

Some pages have prompts for writing and drawing, while others are totally blank. The writing prompts include inspirational readings, thoughts about human interaction and personal reflections. The drawing spaces include a variety of art exercises and ideas to inspire creativity. The rest of the page is blank to be used for creative writing, recording events, sorting out emotions, artwork or whatever you wish.

You can also record such things as exercise, nightly dreams or major current events. Of course, you will make it your own. As you use the journal, you will surely add, delete, edit, augment, and ignore, all as you please.

Don't feel compelled to rigidly follow the guides and prompts. By all means, substitute a favorite phrase or reading for those provided. Cross off or ignore the parts you don't want. Many pages are blank so you can add your own rituals, writings and whatever centers you each day. If you miss a day you can leave it, or go back later and fill it in. Choose whatever direction you wish to make this journal your unique statement.

How to Use This Journal

On first glance, you'll notice this is a unique approach to journaling. What follows is a simple guide explaining the headings and abbreviated references you will find. Some prompts are self-explanatory, and some may cause you to refer back to this section. Remember, these are merely suggestions, and you can use the pages as you wish.

The Writing Prompts

Day: This is at the top of each page. Use this space when you want to break or start a habit, or to record progress toward a goal. For example, if you commit to a 12-week fitness program, write Days 1-84 and then record your progress with the program each day.

Motivational Reading: Choose a passage from one of your favorite motivational books, or flip to a random page. Reflect on what that passage is saying to you on this particular day.

Celebrate accomplishments: Take a moment from time to time to recognize your accomplishments, large and small. Celebrate you!

Prayers: Use the pen and paper to package up a thought for others or yourself, and send it out to your Higher Power to be answered.

Other Prompts: Some will be clear; others may be more mysterious. Write about whatever the prompt inspires in you.

Blank Pages at the End: There are headers as suggestions, but you should use them as you please. You can record big events, keep track of exercise goals, or log reminders and statistics that you want to save from year to year.

The Drawing Boxes

This journal challenges you to exercise your whole brain with daily doodles and drawings. The pages contain drawing prompts to inspire ideas and lead you to naturally fresh ideas every day. Remember, there are no judgments here. Use a pen if you like. Don't bother erasing anything. You're not going to submit these drawings to an art contest. You are simply exploring and working different parts of your brain.

Blind Contour: Look at an object and draw it without looking at your paper (self-control here!). You'll end up with a big funny mess, but you might see a few lines that resemble parts of the subject. The key is to exercise a part of your brain that rarely gets a workout.

Comics: Find the funny pages and copy a few of your favorite characters. Valuable lessons come from talented cartoonists who express a huge range of human feelings with minimal lines.

Mandala: A mandala is a circular pattern often used for meditation and contemplation. Mandalas are often associated with Eastern religions, yet circular patterns can also be found in Native American art and the glass windows of cathedrals. Start with a dot in the center of the blank circle to create your own meditative patterns.

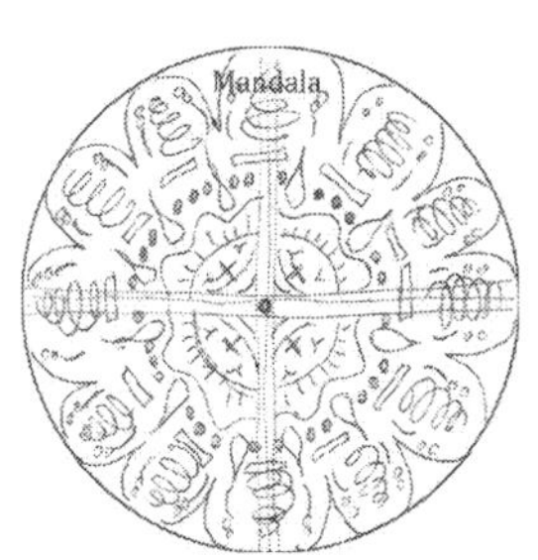

Snow Globe: Create an interesting little scene as if it were captured within a snow globe. Current events often provide ideas for snow globe drawings.

Single-Line: Choose an object to draw and do so without lifting your pen from the paper at all. Not once. Back track, make errant lines, but do not lift the pen. Hmmm… there's a lesson in this activity too.

Words and Phrases: The words and phrases are meant to inspire silly, anything-goes type drawings. This might challenge you to draw from imagination or to tackle human figures (even stick figures). Let your creative streak shine. Seriously, anything goes!

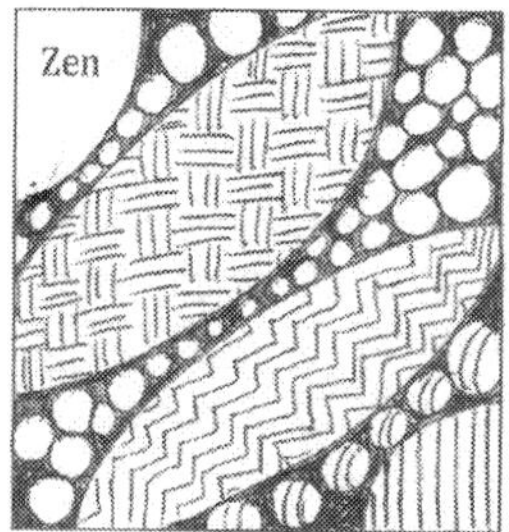

Zen: Draw some simple shapes and then fill in the rest with patterns. Try not to think too hard about it; let your hand do the work freely without your brain interfering too much.

Blank Boxes: Some drawing boxes are long and skinny for making a border; others are square. Of course, use these for whatever you like. Write through them. Enlarge them. Ignore them. It's your journal! Have fun creating!

Doodle: Close your eyes and make some random marks in the space. Then look at what you have done from every angle. Turn the book all around and see what emerges for you. Add as much as you need to complete the drawing.

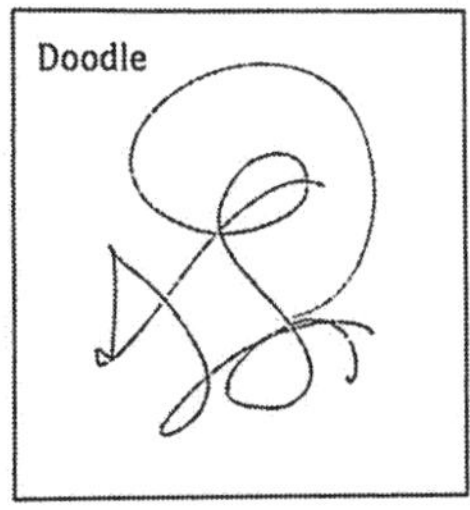

Newspaper Pic: Choose a picture from a newspaper or magazine to copy. Photos on the sports pages are great because arms and legs are often in strange positions. Photos from major current events are also interesting. Again, remember that you are not entering an art contest with this exercise.

It's time to get started!

Resolutions and Goals

Motivational Books

Notes

Notes

January

Day:

1

Resolutions

What if…

Day:

January

2

Gratitude

January

Day:

3

Swimming

Day:

January

4

Blind Contour

January

Day:

5

Bucket List

Day:

January

6

Who needs an extra does of friendliness?

January

Day:

7

Forgiveness. Who needs it from me?

Day:

January

8

Comics

January

Day:

9

Traits of strength I've inherited

Day: January

10

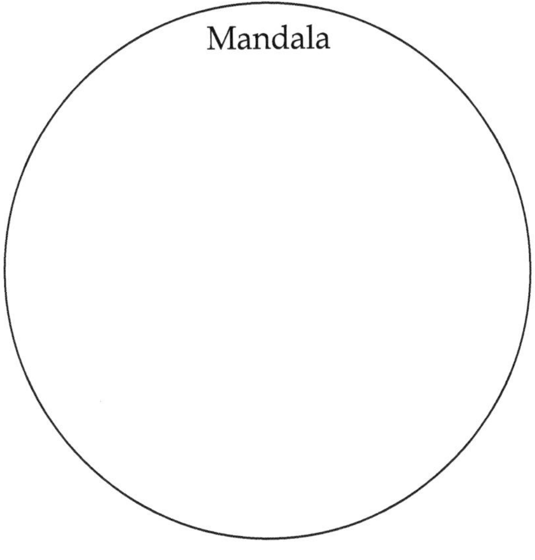

January

Day:

11

Single-Line

Day:

January

12

Celebrate Accomplishments

January

Day:

13

Doodle

Day:

January

14

Prayers

January Day:

15

Motivational Reading

Day: January

16

Happy Birthday

January

Day:

17

Who do I need to ask for forgiveness?

Day: January

18

Uh Oh. Food Fight!

January

Day:

19

Angels in my life...

Day:

January

20

Zen

January

Day:

21

Equality

Day:

January

22

What if this were my last day to live?

January

Day:

23

Day:

January

24

Doodle

January

Day:

25

Gratitude

Day:

January

26

January

Day:

27

Doodle

Day:

January

28

Motivational Reading

January

Day:

29

Newspaper Pic

Day:

January

30

Prayers

January

Day:

31

Doodle

Day: February

1

Prayers

February

Day:

2

Gratitude

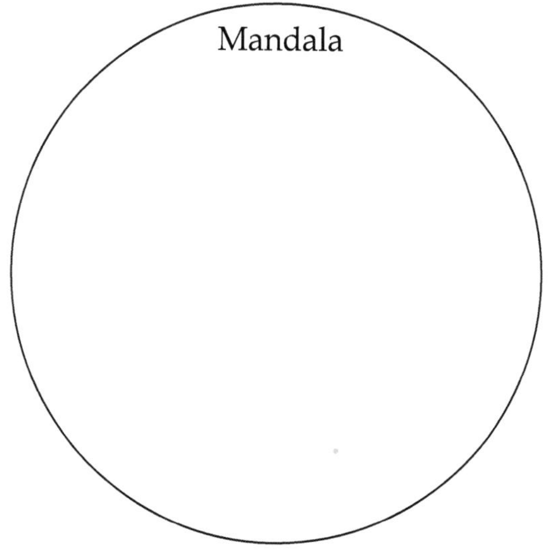

Day:

February

3

February

Day:

4

Blind Contour

Day:

February

5

February

Day:

6

Victory Dance

Day:

February

7

Forgiveness

February

Day:

8

How can I show love to strangers?

Day:

February

9

February

Day:

10

Single-Line

Day:

February

11

Celebrate
Accomplishments

February

Day:

12

Day: **February**

13

Hibernation and the darkness of winter

February

Day:

14

Unconditional Love

Hearts

Day:

February

15

Doodle

February

Day:

16

Jungle

Day:

February

17

How can I better avoid arguments?

February

Day:

18

What makes a great leader?

There's a monster in the shower!

Day:

February

19

February

Day:

20

Zen

Day:

February

21

February

Day:

22

Newspaper Pic

Day:

February

23

How can I pay it forward today?

February

Day:

24

Gratitude

Day:

February

25

Comics

February

Day:

26

Zen

Day:

February

27

Motivational Reading

February

Day:

28

Single-Line

Day:

February

29

LEAP DAY! What would I do with 24 extra unscheduled, unplanned hours???

March

Day:

1

Forgiveness

Day

March

2

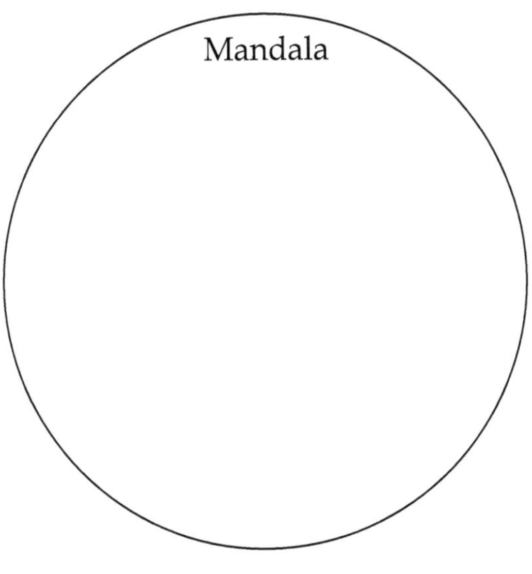

March

Day:

3

Gratitude

Day:

March

4

Blind Contour

March

Day:

5

Quarters

Day:

March

6

How can I better see things from the other's point of view?

March

Day:

7

Day:

March

8

Comics

March

Day:

9

What issue from my past needs healing?

Day:

March

10

Single-Line

March

Day:

11

Bucket List

Day:

March

12

Celebrate Accomplishments

March

Day:

13

Shamrocks

Day: March

14

Doodle

March

Day:

15

How can I work on integrity?

Day:

March

16

March

Day:

17

Luck

Day:

March

18

Take a jet pack to Saturn!

March

Day:

19

Angels in my life...

Day:

March

20

Zen

March

Day:

21

Prayers

Day:

March

22

Newspaper Pic

March

Day:

23

What needs action right now?

Day: March

24

March

Day:

25

Gratitude

Day:

March

26

X-ray Vision

March

Day:

27

Doodle

Day:

March

28

Motivational Reading

March

Day:

29

Where can I create a win-win situation?

Day:

March

30

Prayers

March

Day:

31

Doodle

Day: April

1

Gratitude

April

Day:

2

Day:

April

3

Levitate

April

Day:

4

How can I become a better listener?

Day: *April*

5

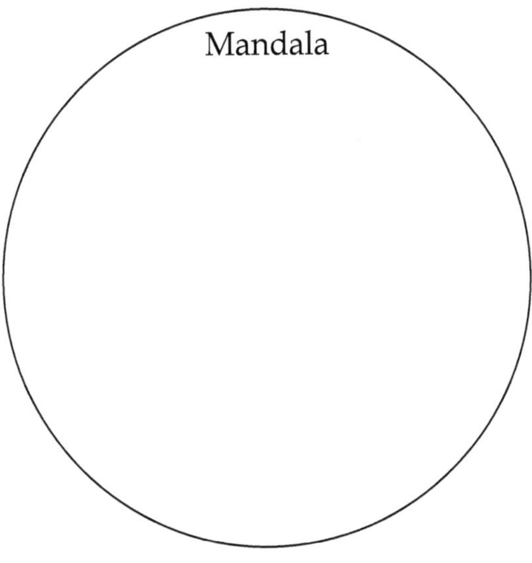

April

Day:

6

Forgiveness

Day: April

7

Make a small change to the routine today.

April

Day:

8

Comics

Day:

April

9

Sacrifice

April

Day:

10

Celebrate Accomplishments

Day:

April

11

Single-Line

April

Day:

12

Day:

April

13

Compassion

April

Day:

14

Day:

April

15

Doodle

April

Day:

16

How can I be of service to others?

Day:

April

17

Zeppelin

April

Day:

18

Day:

April

19

Prayers

Everything is better with chocolate syrup.

April

Day:

20

How can I keep my sense of humor?

Day:

April

21

Zen

April

Day:

22

Newspaper Pic

Day: April

23

April

Day:

24

Gratitude

Day: April

25

Blind Contour

April

Day:

26

Motivational Reading

Day:

April

27

Doodle

April

Day:

28

Day:

April

29

Single-Line

April

Day:

30

Revisit Resolutions

Day:

May

1

Prayers

May

Day:

2

Gratitude

Day:

May

3

Blind Contour

May

Day:

4

Day:

May

5

Do I need to admit to someone that I've been wrong?

May

Day:

6

Nurturing

Flowers

Day:

May

7

Forgiveness

May

Day:

8

How can I become more centered and balanced?

Day:

May

9

Comics

May

Day:

10

Day:

May

11

Celebrate
Accomplishments

May

Day:

12

Single-Line

Day:

May

13

Doodle

May

Day:

14

Magical Moments

Day:

May

15

I'm taking my pet shark for a walk.

May

Day:

16

Day: May

17

Who needs me to show more appreciation?

May

Day:

18

Push and Pull

Day:

May

19

Zen

May

Day:

20

Prayers

Day:

May

21

Wisdom

May

Day:

22

Newspaper Pic

Day:

May

23

May

Day:

24

Gratitude

Day: *May*

25

Doodle

May

Day:

26

Patriotism

Day:

May

27

Motivational Reading

May

Day:

28

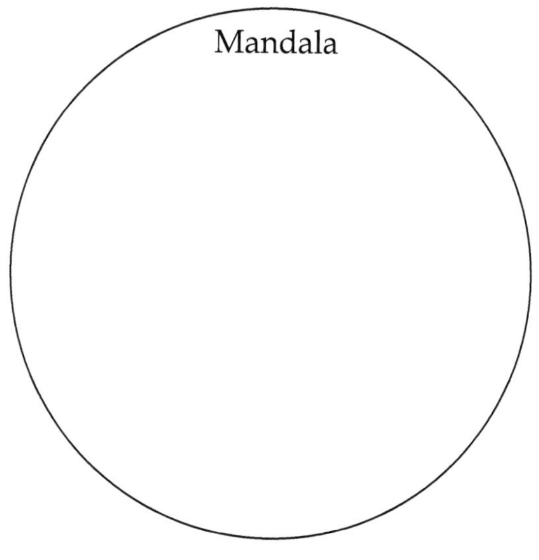

Day: May

29

Prayers

May

Day:

30

Bursting

Day:

May

31

Angels in my life...

June

Day:

1

Gratitude

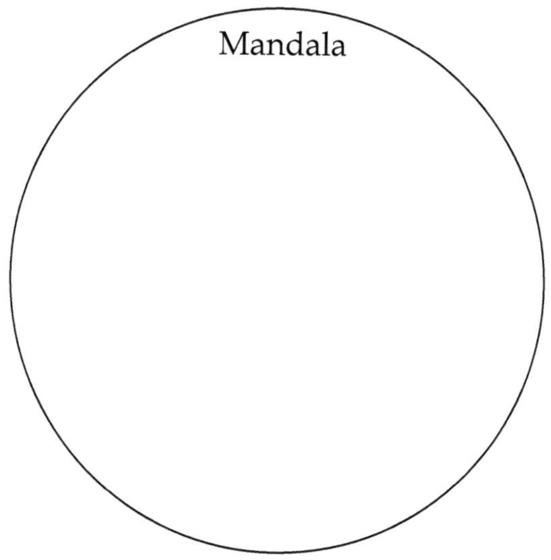

Day:

June

2

June

Day:

3

Blind Contour

Day:

June

4

What am I being called to do?

June

Day:

5

Hysterical

Day:

June

6

Forgiveness

June

Day:

7

Staying present in the moment

Day:

June

8

Comics

June

Day:

9

Day:

June

10

Celebrate Accomplishments

June

Day:

11

Single-Line

Day:

June

12

June

Day:

13

Mastering My Emotions

Day:

June

14

Self-Discipline

June

Day:

15

Doodle

Day: June

16

Whose spirits can I boost?

June

Day:

17

Geography

Day:

June

18

June

Day:

19

Prayers

Day:

June

20

Persistence

June

Day:

21

Zen

Day:

June

22

Traveling and Exploring

Newspaper Pic

June

Day:

23

Gratitude

Day:

June

24

Oh no! The ______ has exploded!

June

Day:

25

Day: June

26

Motivational Reading

June

Day:

27

Bucket List

Day:

June

28

June

Day:

29

Oh, if money were no object!

Day: June

30

Doodle

July

Day:

1

Prayers

Day:

July

2

Gratitude

July

Day:

3

Wrecking

Day:

July

4

Freedom

July

Day:

5

Letting someone else save face

Day:

July

6

Blind Contour

July

Day:

7

Comics

Day: **July**

8

What favor can I pay forward?

July

Day:

9

Day:

July

10

Forgiveness

July Day:

11

Single-Line

Day:

July

12

Celebrate Accomplishments

July

Day:

13

I can balance a ______ on my nose.

Day:

July

14

Inner Strength

July

Day:

15

Doodle

Day:

July

16

Crawling

July

Day:

17

Balance in Life

Day:

July

18

July

Day:

19

Zen

Day:

July

20

Prayers

July

Day:

21

Day:

July

22

Newspaper Pic

July

Day:

23

Day:

July

24

Gratitude

July Day:

25

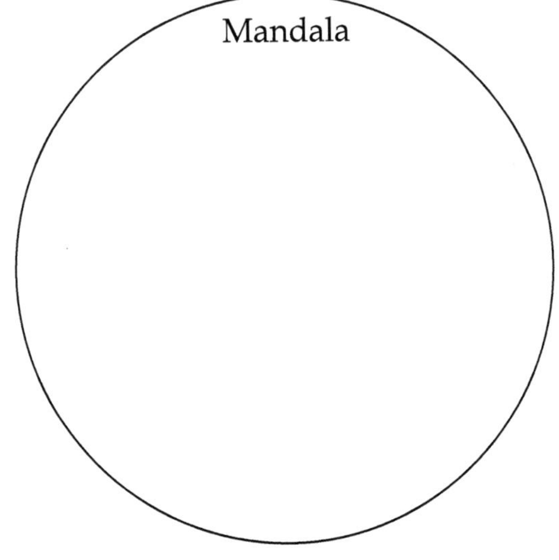

Day:

July

26

Motivational
Reading

July

Day:

27

Doodle

Day:

July

28

How can I increase my impact on the world?

July

Day:

29

Prayers

Day:

July

30

Doodle

July

Day:

31

Prayers

Day:

August

1

Gratitude

August

Day:

2

Ominous

Day:

August

3

Relax and let go of it

August

Day:

4

Lay down a challenge

Day:

August

5

Blind Contour

August

Day:

6

Day: August

7

Trust

August

Day:

8

Angels in my life...

Day: **August**

9

Comics

August

Day:

10

Celebrate Accomplishments

Day: **August**

11

Forgiveness

Single-Line

August

Day:

12

Day: August

13

Insight

August

Day:

14

Day:

August

15

Doodle

August

Day:

16

Commitment

Day: August

17

Loose

August

Day:

18

What if people were made of _________?

Day: **August**

19

Prayers

August

Day:

20

Mastering my emotions

Day: August

21

Zen

August

Day:

22

Newspaper Pic

Day: August

23

August

Day:

24

Gratitude

Day: **August**

25

Dropping

August

Day:

26

Motivational Reading

Day:

August

27

Umbrellas

August

Day:

28

Day:

August

29

Prayers

August

Day:

30

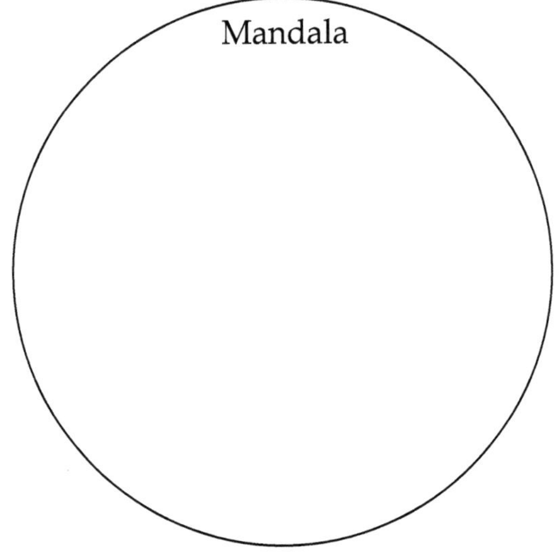

Day:

August

31

September

Day:

1

Gratitude

Day: September

2

September

Day:

3

Camping

Day: September

4

Finding common ground

Blind Contour

September

Day:

5

Angels in my life...

Day:

September

6

Doodle

September

Day:

7

Wisdom and honoring elders

Day:

September 8

Comics

September

Day:

9

Day:

September

10

Celebrate

Accomplishments

September *Day:*

11

Single-Line

Day:

September

12

Forgiveness

September

Day:

13

Creating

Day:

September

14

Doodle

September

Day:

15

Yodeling

Day: September

16

How can I be a better listener?

September

Day:

17

Renewal

Day: September

18

Look, the ______ learned how to pole vault.

September Day:

19

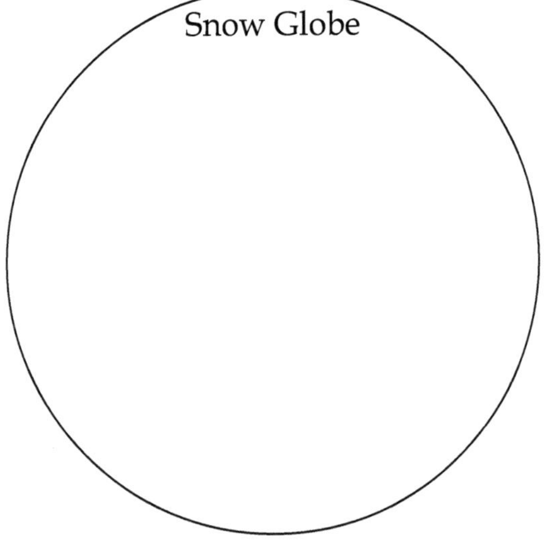

Day:

September 20

My Unique Strengths

September

Day:

21

Happy Birthday

Day:

September

22

Newspaper Pic

September

Day:

23

Gratitude

Day:

September

24

Zen

September

Day:

25

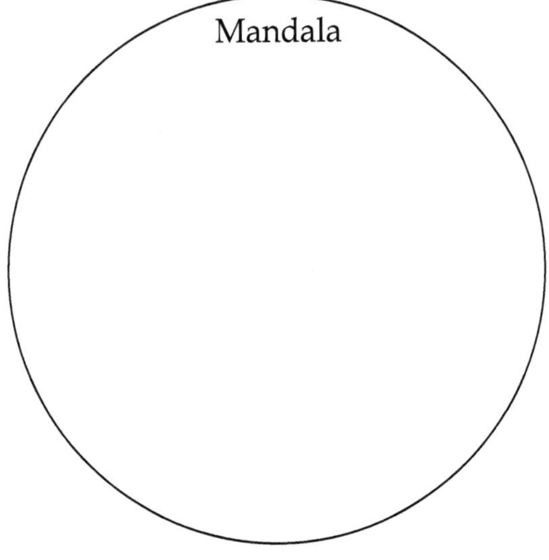

Day:

September 26

Motivational Reading

September

Day:

27

Doodle

Day:

September

28

Single-Line

September

Day:

29

Revisit Resolutions

Day:

September

30

Flimsy

October

Day:

1

Prayers

Day:

October

2

October

Day:

3

Gratitude

Day:

October

4

Blind Contour

October

Day:

5

What if I knew that this were someone else's last day to live?

Day: October

6

October

Day:

7

Comics

Day:

October

8

Five things I like about myself

October Day:

9

Risky

Day: October

10

Forgiveness

October

Day:

11

Celebrate Accomplishments

Day: October

12

Single-Line

October

Day:

13

Taking Risks

Day:

October

14

Release

October

Day:

15

Facing Fears

Day:

October

16

Doodle

October

Day:

17

Reputation

Day:

October

18

I can't believe I ate the whole _______.

October

Day:

19

Bucket List

Day:

October

20

Zen

October Day:

21

Day:

October

22

Newspaper Pic

October

Day:

23

Lessons Learned

Day:

October

24

Gratitude

October

Day:

25

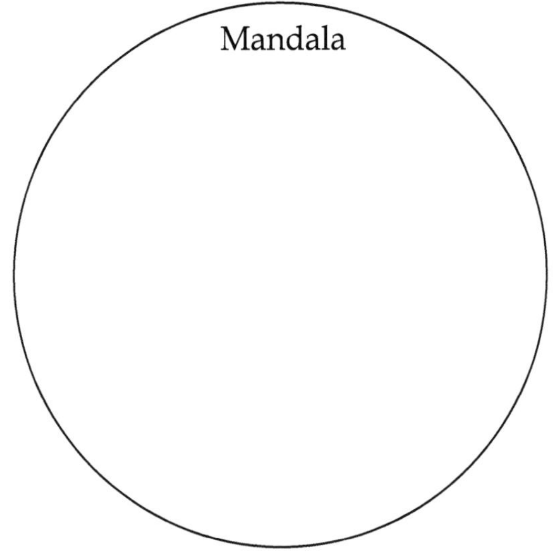

Day: October

26

October

Day:

27

Motivational Reading

Day:

October

28

Ice Cream

October

Day:

29

Doodle

Day:

October

30

October

Day:

31

Halloween

Day:

November

1

Angels in my life:

Angels

November

Day:

2

Gratitude

Day: November

3

Happy Birthday

November

Day:

4

Bucket List

Day:

November

5

Blind Contour

November

Day:

6

Messy

Day: November

7

Gifts I have to give

November

Day:

8

Comics

Day:

November

9

Celebrate Accomplishments

November

Day:

10

Anniversary

Day: # November

11

Veterans' Day

November

Day:

12

Remembering those who are gone

Single-Line

Day: November

13

Healing

November

Day:

14

Gratitude

Day:

November

15

Doodle

November

Day:

16

Noble

Day: November

17

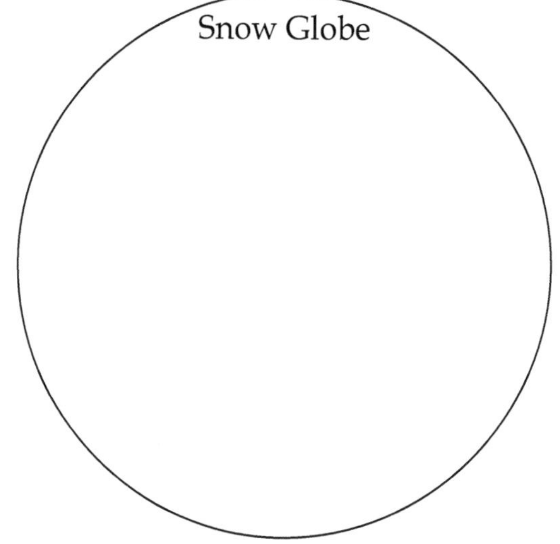

November

Day:

18

Forgiveness

Day:

November

19

Someone got a terrible haircut!

November

Day:

20

Radiating Enthusiasm

Day:

November

21

Zen

November

Day:

22

Newspaper Pic

Day: November

23

Gratitude

November

Day:

24

Day: November

25

Happy Birthday

November

Day:

26

Motivational Reading

Day: November

27

Toppling

November

Day:

28

What problem needs solving?

Day: November

29

November Day:

30

Prayers

Day:

December

1

Mandala

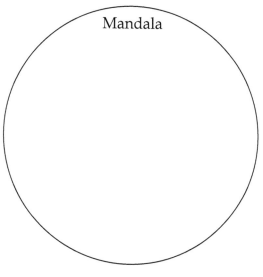

December

Day:

2

Gratitude

Day:

December

3

Year in Review

December

Day:

4

Surrender: Let go of something

Day: December

5

Blind Contour

December

Day:

6

Aim

Day: December

7

Embracing the Unpredictable

December

Day:

8

You can't skydive with a __________.

Day:

December

9

December

Day:

10

Celebrate
Accomplishments

Day:

December

11

Single-Line

December

Day:

12

Day:

December

13

Connect

December

Day:

14

Day:

December

15

Doodle

December

Day:

16

Day:

December

17

December

Day:

18

Kites

Day:

December

19

Prayers

December

Day:

20

Keeping a sense of humor

Day:

December

21

Zen

December

Day:

22

Newspaper Pic

Day: December

23

Gratitude

December Day:

24

Day:

December

25

Pondering Miracles

December

Day:

26

Blind Contour

Day:

December

27

Doodle

December

Day:

28

Imagination

Day: December

29

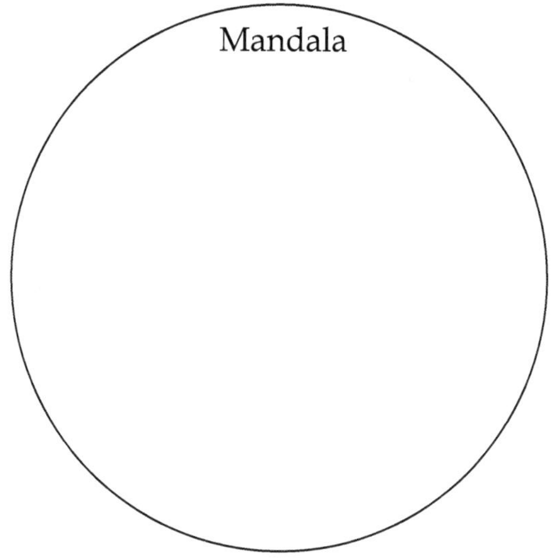

December

Day:

30

Unfinished Business

Day:

December

31

Revisit Resolutions

Notes

Dreams

Visions

Plans

Inspirations

Aspirations

Memories

Year in Review

Unfinished Business

Notes

Made in the USA
Charleston, SC
30 November 2013